PLASTIC-FREE year
Journal for kids

Save the ocean
Monthly weekly planner

by ECOKIDOS
2019

This notebook belongs to:

Year_____

Be the change
you wish to see in the world.
                    - Mahatma Gandhi

PLASTIC IS EVERYWHERE.

Did you know that According to some estimates, if we continue on our current path, the oceans will contain more plastic than fish by the year 2050?

We've produced as much plastic in the past decade as we did in the entire twentieth century. We're drowning in the stuff, and we need to start making some hard choices.

There are thousands of books that explain why not to use plastic or to have a zero-waste life, but the truth is that none of those books actually get you into action.

This planner is made for you to start changing the world from today.

In this book, you will find:

1. Tips on how to live life without plastic.

2. Guided templates to fill with your plastic-free plan for:
- Toys
- Sweet time
- Emails
- Christmas time
- Books and blogs
- Party decorations
- Plastic counter

3. Monthly planner

4. Weekly planner

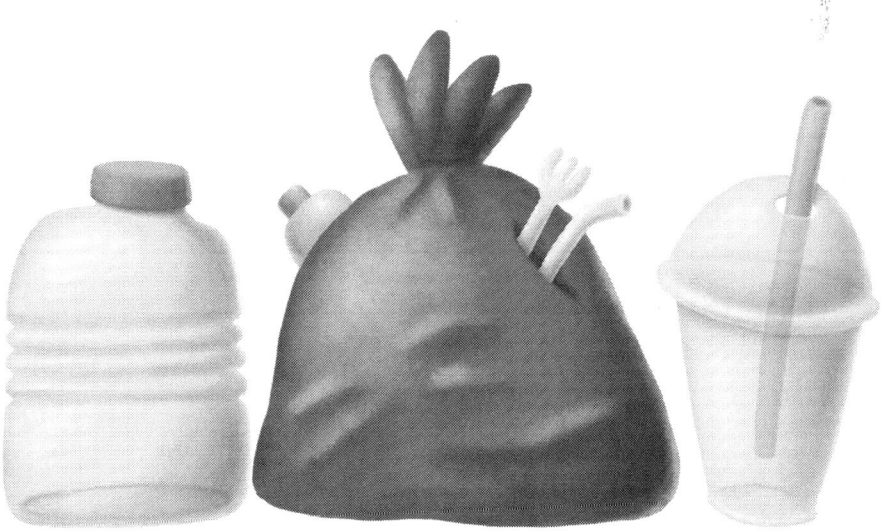

EVERY SMALL STEP MATTERS WHEN IT IS RELATED TO REDUCING PLASTIC WASTE. START TODAY!

ECO TOYS

List of toys that don't harm the earth

_____

_____

_____

_____

_____

_____

_____

_____

_____

_____

_____

_____

_____

_____

_____

_____

_____

_____

_____

_____

_____

_____

_____

_____

_____

SWEET TIME!

Ideas for Plastic-free desserts

_____

_____

_____

_____

_____

_____

_____

_____

_____

_____

_____

_____

_____

_____

_____

_____

_____

_____

_____

_____

_____

_____

EMAILS

Sent to ask companies to save the world:

I.e.: to change packaging
Ask for transparency of ingredients...

Date	To

LEARN MORE

About living a Plastic-free life

Books to read

_____

_____

_____

_____

_____

_____

_____

_____

_____

_____

_____

_____

Blogs to follow

_____

_____

_____

_____

_____

_____

_____

_____

_____

_____

_____

_____

CHRISTMAS TIME!

Tree decoration ideas

_____

_____

_____

_____

_____

_____

_____

_____

_____

_____

_____

_____

_____

_____

_____

_____

_____

_____

_____

_____

_____

PARTY DECORATIONS

Ideas of recycled ornaments

TRAVEL

Tips on traveling a Plastic-free

_____
_____
_____
_____
_____
_____
_____
_____
_____
_____
_____
_____
_____
_____
_____

_____
_____
_____
_____
_____
_____
_____
_____
_____
_____
_____
_____
_____
_____
_____

PLASTIC COUNTER

Pick a random day and count how many times you use single-use plastic

TIPS ON HOW TO LIVE PLASTIC-FREE:

- Give up gum. Gum is made of a synthetic rubber, aka plastic.

- Ask companies to change their packaging

- Choose wooden toys instead of plastic

- Choose reusable cloth sandwich/snack bags

- Choose stainless steel ice cube trays and Popsicle molds

- Avoid disposable plastic pens

- Throw a zero-waste party

- Consider giving charitable gift cards

- Find ways to wrap gifts without plastic tape

- Buy second-hand toys

- Bring your own cup

- Say no to plastic straws

- Start your own plastic-free campaign

- Carry reusable shopping bags

- Treat yourself to an ice cream cone

- Buy fresh bread that comes in either paper bags or no bags

- Support small and local businesses

- Switch to bar soap instead of liquid soap

- Tell your friends that you want to save the planet

MONTHLY PLANNER

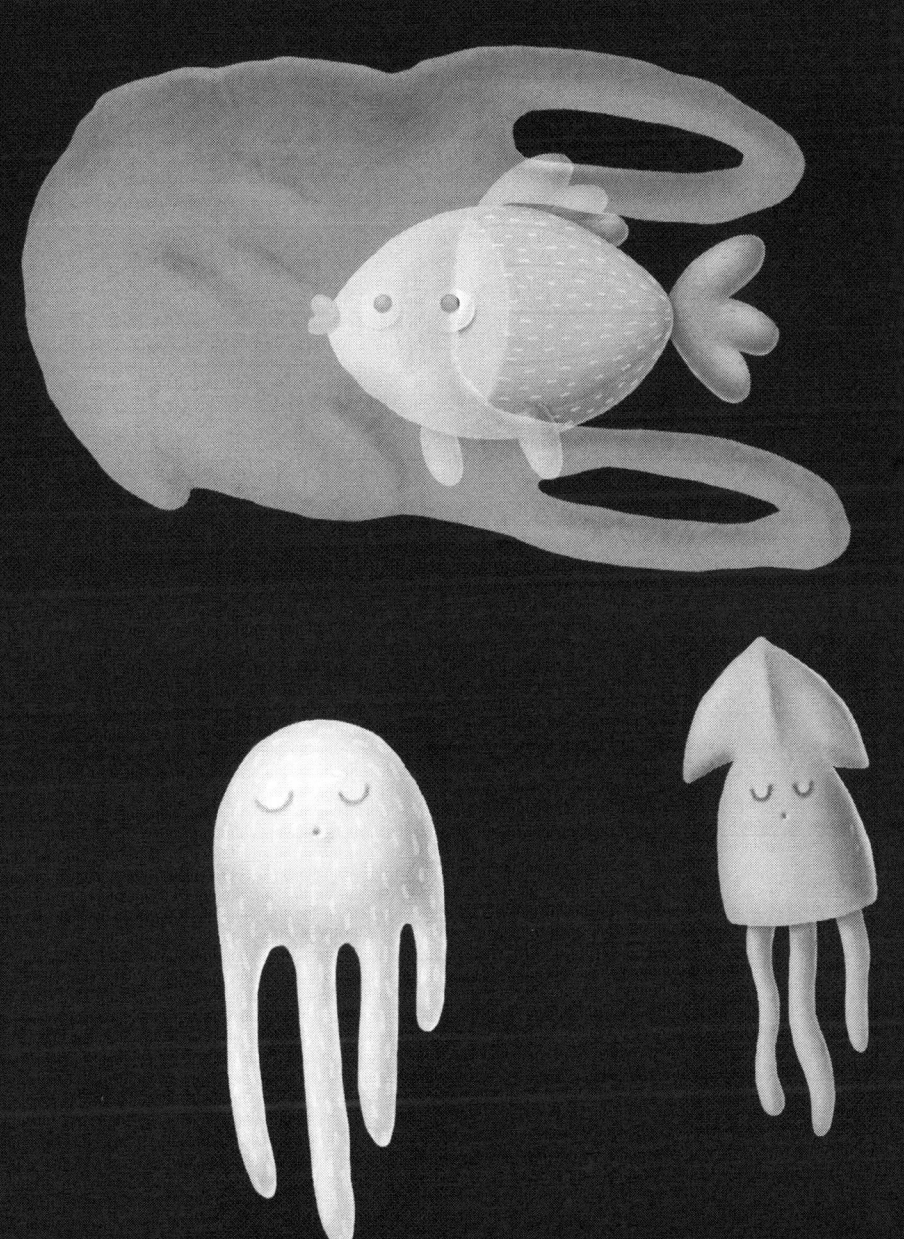

NOTES

MONTH:_____

SUN	MON	TUE	WED	THU	FRI	SAT

NOTES

_____   _____
_____   _____
_____   _____
_____   _____
_____   _____
_____   _____
_____   _____
_____   _____
_____   _____
_____   _____
_____   _____
_____   _____
_____   _____
_____   _____
_____   _____
_____   _____

MONTH:_____

SUN	MON	TUE	WED	THU	FRI	SAT

NOTES

MONTH:_____

SUN	MON	TUE	WED	THU	FRI	SAT

NOTES

MONTH:_____

SUN	MON	TUE	WED	THU	FRI	SAT

NOTES

MONTH:_____

SUN	MON	TUE	WED	THU	FRI	SAT

NOTES

MONTH:_____

SUN	MON	TUE	WED	THU	FRI	SAT

NOTES

MONTH:_____

SUN	MON	TUE	WED	THU	FRI	SAT

NOTES

MONTH:_____

SUN	MON	TUE	WED	THU	FRI	SAT

NOTES

MONTH:_____

SUN	MON	TUE	WED	THU	FRI	SAT

NOTES

MONTH:_____

SUN	MON	TUE	WED	THU	FRI	SAT

NOTES

MONTH:_____

SUN	MON	TUE	WED	THU	FRI	SAT

NOTES

MONTH:_____

SUN	MON	TUE	WED	THU	FRI	SAT

NOTES

WEEKLY PLANNER

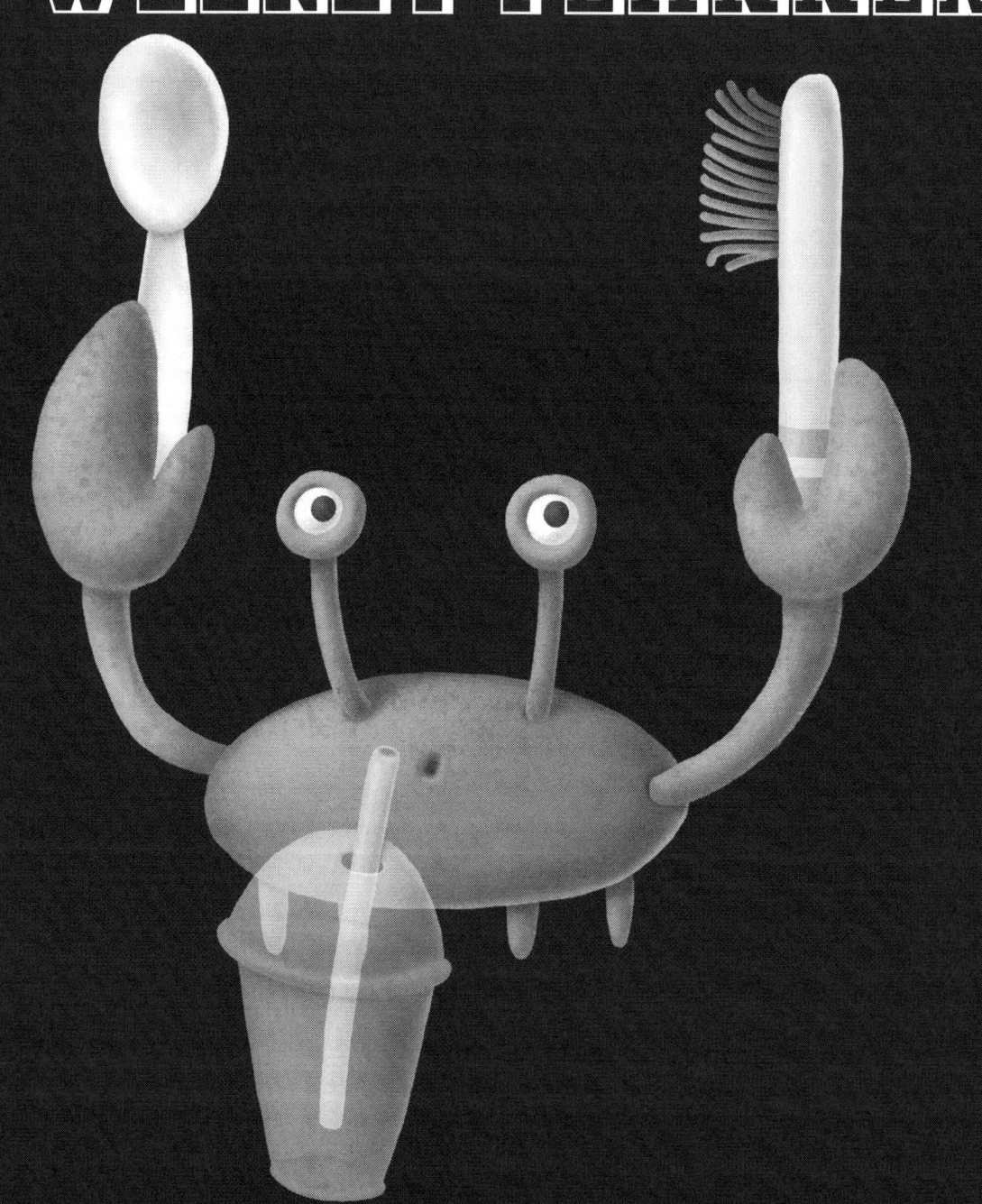

○ MONDAY

PLASTIC-FREE ACTIONS

○ TUESDAY

○ WEDNESDAY

TO DO

○ THURSDAY

○ FRIDAY

○ SATURDAY / SUNDAY

○ MONDAY

PLASTIC-FREE ACTIONS

○ TUESDAY

○ WEDNESDAY

TO DO

○ THURSDAY

○ FRIDAY

○ SATURDAY / SUNDAY

○ MONDAY

PLASTIC-FREE ACTIONS

○ TUESDAY

○ WEDNESDAY

TO DO

○ THURSDAY

○ FRIDAY

○ SATURDAY / SUNDAY

○ MONDAY

PLASTIC-FREE ACTIONS

○ TUESDAY

○ WEDNESDAY

TO DO

○ THURSDAY

○ FRIDAY

○ SATURDAY / SUNDAY

○ MONDAY

PLASTIC-FREE ACTIONS

○ TUESDAY

○ WEDNESDAY

TO DO

○ THURSDAY

○ FRIDAY

○ SATURDAY / SUNDAY

○ MONDAY

PLASTIC-FREE ACTIONS

○ TUESDAY

○ WEDNESDAY

TO DO

○ THURSDAY

○ FRIDAY

○ SATURDAY / SUNDAY

○ MONDAY

PLASTIC-FREE ACTIONS

○ TUESDAY

○ WEDNESDAY

TO DO

○ THURSDAY

○ FRIDAY

○ SATURDAY / SUNDAY

○ MONDAY

PLASTIC-FREE ACTIONS

_____

_____

_____

_____

_____

_____

○ TUESDAY

○ WEDNESDAY

TO DO

_____

_____

_____

_____

○ THURSDAY

_____

_____

_____

_____

○ FRIDAY

_____

_____

_____

_____

○ SATURDAY / SUNDAY

_____

_____

_____

○ MONDAY

PLASTIC-FREE ACTIONS

○ TUESDAY

○ WEDNESDAY

TO DO

○ THURSDAY

○ FRIDAY

○ SATURDAY / SUNDAY

○ MONDAY

PLASTIC-FREE ACTIONS

○ TUESDAY

○ WEDNESDAY

TO DO

○ THURSDAY

○ FRIDAY

○ SATURDAY / SUNDAY

○ MONDAY

PLASTIC-FREE ACTIONS

○ TUESDAY

○ WEDNESDAY

TO DO

○ THURSDAY

○ FRIDAY

○ SATURDAY / SUNDAY

○ MONDAY

PLASTIC-FREE ACTIONS

_____

_____

_____

○ TUESDAY

_____

_____

_____

_____

○ WEDNESDAY

TO DO

_____

_____

○ THURSDAY

_____

_____

_____

_____

○ FRIDAY

_____

_____

_____

_____

○ SATURDAY / SUNDAY

_____

_____

_____

_____

○ MONDAY

PLASTIC-FREE ACTIONS

○ TUESDAY

○ WEDNESDAY

TO DO

○ THURSDAY

○ FRIDAY

○ SATURDAY / SUNDAY

○ MONDAY

PLASTIC-FREE ACTIONS

○ TUESDAY

○ WEDNESDAY

TO DO

○ THURSDAY

○ FRIDAY

○ SATURDAY / SUNDAY

○ MONDAY

PLASTIC-FREE ACTIONS

○ TUESDAY

○ WEDNESDAY

TO DO

○ THURSDAY

○ FRIDAY

○ SATURDAY / SUNDAY

○ MONDAY

PLASTIC-FREE ACTIONS

○ TUESDAY

○ WEDNESDAY

TO DO

○ THURSDAY

○ FRIDAY

○ SATURDAY / SUNDAY

○ MONDAY

PLASTIC-FREE ACTIONS

○ TUESDAY

○ WEDNESDAY

TO DO

○ THURSDAY

○ FRIDAY

○ SATURDAY / SUNDAY

○ MONDAY

PLASTIC-FREE ACTIONS

○ TUESDAY

○ WEDNESDAY

TO DO

○ THURSDAY

○ FRIDAY

○ SATURDAY / SUNDAY

○ MONDAY

PLASTIC-FREE ACTIONS

_____

_____

○ TUESDAY

_____

_____

_____

_____

○ WEDNESDAY

TO DO

_____

○ THURSDAY

_____

_____

_____

_____

○ FRIDAY

_____

_____

_____

○ SATURDAY / SUNDAY

_____

_____

_____

_____

○ MONDAY

PLASTIC-FREE ACTIONS

○ TUESDAY

○ WEDNESDAY

TO DO

○ THURSDAY

○ FRIDAY

○ SATURDAY / SUNDAY

○ MONDAY

PLASTIC-FREE ACTIONS

○ TUESDAY

○ WEDNESDAY

TO DO

○ THURSDAY

○ FRIDAY

○ SATURDAY / SUNDAY

○ MONDAY

PLASTIC-FREE ACTIONS

○ TUESDAY

○ WEDNESDAY

TO DO

○ THURSDAY

○ FRIDAY

○ SATURDAY / SUNDAY

○ MONDAY

PLASTIC-FREE ACTIONS

○ TUESDAY

○ WEDNESDAY

TO DO

○ THURSDAY

○ FRIDAY

○ SATURDAY / SUNDAY

○ MONDAY

PLASTIC-FREE ACTIONS

_____

_____

_____

○ TUESDAY

_____

_____

_____

○ WEDNESDAY

TO DO

_____

_____

_____

○ THURSDAY

_____

_____

_____

○ FRIDAY

_____

_____

_____

○ SATURDAY / SUNDAY

_____

_____

_____

○ MONDAY

PLASTIC-FREE ACTIONS

○ TUESDAY

○ WEDNESDAY

TO DO

○ THURSDAY

○ FRIDAY

○ SATURDAY / SUNDAY

○ MONDAY

PLASTIC-FREE ACTIONS

○ TUESDAY

○ WEDNESDAY

TO DO

○ THURSDAY

○ FRIDAY

○ SATURDAY / SUNDAY

○ MONDAY

PLASTIC-FREE ACTIONS

○ TUESDAY

○ WEDNESDAY

TO DO

○ THURSDAY

○ FRIDAY

○ SATURDAY / SUNDAY

○ MONDAY

PLASTIC-FREE ACTIONS

_____

_____

_____

○ TUESDAY

_____

_____

_____

_____

○ WEDNESDAY

TO DO

_____

_____

_____

○ THURSDAY

_____

_____

_____

_____

○ FRIDAY

_____

_____

_____

_____

○ SATURDAY / SUNDAY

_____

_____

_____

○ MONDAY

PLASTIC-FREE ACTIONS

_____

_____

○ TUESDAY

_____

_____

_____

_____

_____

○ WEDNESDAY

TO DO

_____

_____

○ THURSDAY

_____

_____

_____

_____

○ FRIDAY

_____

_____

_____

_____

○ SATURDAY / SUNDAY

_____

_____

_____

○ MONDAY

PLASTIC-FREE ACTIONS

○ TUESDAY

○ WEDNESDAY

TO DO

○ THURSDAY

○ FRIDAY

○ SATURDAY / SUNDAY

○ MONDAY

PLASTIC-FREE ACTIONS

○ TUESDAY

○ WEDNESDAY

TO DO

○ THURSDAY

○ FRIDAY

○ SATURDAY / SUNDAY

○ MONDAY

PLASTIC-FREE ACTIONS

_____
_____
_____
_____
_____

○ TUESDAY

○ WEDNESDAY

TO DO

_____
_____
_____
_____
_____
_____

○ THURSDAY

○ FRIDAY

_____
_____
_____
_____

○ SATURDAY / SUNDAY

_____
_____

○ MONDAY

PLASTIC-FREE ACTIONS

_____

_____

○ TUESDAY

_____

_____

_____

_____

○ WEDNESDAY

TO DO

_____

_____

○ THURSDAY

_____

_____

_____

_____

○ FRIDAY

_____

_____

_____

_____

○ SATURDAY / SUNDAY

_____

_____

_____

○ MONDAY

PLASTIC-FREE ACTIONS

○ TUESDAY

○ WEDNESDAY

TO DO

○ THURSDAY

○ FRIDAY

○ SATURDAY / SUNDAY

○ MONDAY

PLASTIC-FREE ACTIONS

○ TUESDAY

○ WEDNESDAY

TO DO

○ THURSDAY

○ FRIDAY

○ SATURDAY / SUNDAY

○ MONDAY

PLASTIC-FREE ACTIONS

○ TUESDAY

○ WEDNESDAY

TO DO

○ THURSDAY

○ FRIDAY

○ SATURDAY / SUNDAY

○ MONDAY

PLASTIC-FREE ACTIONS

○ TUESDAY

○ WEDNESDAY

TO DO

○ THURSDAY

○ FRIDAY

○ SATURDAY / SUNDAY

○ MONDAY

PLASTIC-FREE ACTIONS

○ TUESDAY

○ WEDNESDAY

TO DO

○ THURSDAY

○ FRIDAY

○ SATURDAY / SUNDAY

○ MONDAY

PLASTIC-FREE ACTIONS

○ TUESDAY

○ WEDNESDAY

TO DO

○ THURSDAY

○ FRIDAY

○ SATURDAY / SUNDAY

○ MONDAY

PLASTIC-FREE ACTIONS

_____

_____

○ TUESDAY

_____

_____

_____

○ WEDNESDAY

TO DO

_____

_____

○ THURSDAY

_____

_____

_____

○ FRIDAY

_____

_____

_____

○ SATURDAY / SUNDAY

_____

_____

_____

○ MONDAY

PLASTIC-FREE ACTIONS

○ TUESDAY

○ WEDNESDAY

TO DO

○ THURSDAY

○ FRIDAY

○ SATURDAY / SUNDAY

○ MONDAY

PLASTIC-FREE ACTIONS

○ TUESDAY

○ WEDNESDAY

TO DO

○ THURSDAY

○ FRIDAY

○ SATURDAY / SUNDAY

○ MONDAY

PLASTIC-FREE ACTIONS

_____

○ TUESDAY

_____

_____

_____

_____

○ WEDNESDAY

TO DO

_____

○ THURSDAY

_____

_____

_____

_____

○ FRIDAY

_____

_____

_____

○ SATURDAY / SUNDAY

_____

_____

_____

○ MONDAY

PLASTIC-FREE ACTIONS

○ TUESDAY

○ WEDNESDAY

TO DO

○ THURSDAY

○ FRIDAY

○ SATURDAY / SUNDAY

○ MONDAY

PLASTIC-FREE ACTIONS

○ TUESDAY

○ WEDNESDAY

TO DO

○ THURSDAY

○ FRIDAY

○ SATURDAY / SUNDAY

○ MONDAY

PLASTIC-FREE ACTIONS

_____
_____
_____
_____
_____
_____

○ TUESDAY

○ WEDNESDAY

TO DO

_____
_____
_____
_____
_____
_____

○ THURSDAY

○ FRIDAY

_____
_____
_____
_____
_____

○ SATURDAY / SUNDAY

_____
_____
_____

○ MONDAY

PLASTIC-FREE ACTIONS

_____

_____

○ TUESDAY

_____

_____

_____

_____

○ WEDNESDAY

TO DO

_____

_____

○ THURSDAY

_____

_____

_____

_____

○ FRIDAY

_____

_____

_____

_____

○ SATURDAY / SUNDAY

_____

_____

_____

○ MONDAY

PLASTIC-FREE ACTIONS

○ TUESDAY

○ WEDNESDAY

TO DO

○ THURSDAY

○ FRIDAY

○ SATURDAY / SUNDAY

○ MONDAY

PLASTIC-FREE ACTIONS

○ TUESDAY

○ WEDNESDAY

TO DO

○ THURSDAY

○ FRIDAY

○ SATURDAY / SUNDAY

○ MONDAY

PLASTIC-FREE ACTIONS

○ TUESDAY

○ WEDNESDAY

TO DO

○ THURSDAY

○ FRIDAY

○ SATURDAY / SUNDAY

○ MONDAY

PLASTIC-FREE ACTIONS

○ TUESDAY

○ WEDNESDAY

TO DO

○ THURSDAY

○ FRIDAY

○ SATURDAY / SUNDAY

○ MONDAY

PLASTIC-FREE ACTIONS

○ TUESDAY

○ WEDNESDAY

TO DO

○ THURSDAY

○ FRIDAY

○ SATURDAY / SUNDAY

○ MONDAY

PLASTIC-FREE ACTIONS

_____

○ TUESDAY

_____

_____

_____

_____

○ WEDNESDAY

TO DO

_____

○ THURSDAY

_____

_____

_____

_____

○ FRIDAY

_____

_____

_____

_____

○ SATURDAY / SUNDAY

_____

_____

_____